BOARD GAME BUILDER

BUILDER

Milton Bradley

LEE SLATER

**Checkerboard
Library**

An Imprint of Abdo Publishing
abdopublishing.com

abdopublishing.com

Published by Abdo Publishing, a division of ABDO, PO Box 398166, Minneapolis, Minnesota 55439. Copyright © 2016 by Abdo Consulting Group, Inc. International copyrights reserved in all countries. No part of this book may be reproduced in any form without written permission from the publisher. Checkerboard Library™ is a trademark and logo of Abdo Publishing.

Printed in the United States of America, North Mankato, Minnesota
102015
012016

THIS BOOK CONTAINS
RECYCLED MATERIALS

Content Developer: Nancy Tuminelly
Design and Production: Mighty Media, Inc.
Series Editor: Paige Polinsky
Cover Photos: Mighty Media (border); Wikimedia Commons (center)
Interior Photos: Alamy, pp. 16, 22; Courtesy of the Library of Congress, p. 15; Courtesy of the Library of Congress, LC-USZ62-37423, p. 21; Granger, p. 11, p. 28 (top right); New York Public Library/Science Source, p. 9; Shutterstock, pp. 5, 7, 8, 12, 13, 19, 23, 25, 26, 27, 28 (bottom left), 29 (bottom left); Wikimedia Commons, pp. 4, 17.

Library of Congress Control Number: 2015030428
Cataloging-in-Publication Data
Slater, Lee.
 Board game builder: Milton Bradley / Lee Slater.
   p. cm. -- (Toy trailblazers)
 ISBN 978-1-62403-975-1 (lib. bdg.)
 Includes bibliographical references and index.
 1. Bradley, Milton, 1836-1911--Biography--Juvenile literature. 2. Milton Bradley Company--Juvenile literature. 3. Toymakers--United States--History--Juvenile literature.   I. Title.
 688.7/2/092--dc23

                                                    2015030428

CONTENTS

Chapter 1

A LIFE OF WORK
and Play Begins

Milton Bradley was born on November 8, 1836, in Vienna, Maine. Milton's lifetime saw many changes. When he was born, the **Industrial Revolution** had started in the United States. He was an adult when the **Civil War** began. Just before the war, he started a **revolutionary** game company that would change playtime forever.

During the mid-1800s, many people were moving from farms to cities. They were looking for a new way of life. Milton's family moved five times while he was growing up. The Bradleys

Milton Bradley combined work and play from a very young age and became a successful businessman.

finally settled in Lowell, Massachusetts. There, Milton's father, Lewis, worked in a **textile mill**.

Lewis sometimes helped his son with his homework. He gave Milton objects such as apples to use to help him solve math problems. This made homework feel more like play than work.

Milton continued to mix work and play for the rest of his life. Today, more than 100 fun and successful board games bear his name. Chances are you, your parents, grandparents, and even great-grandparents have all played Milton Bradley games!

Chapter 2
A YOUNG MAN
with Bright Ideas

In the early 1850s, Bradley attended Lowell High School. There, he met George Tapley. Tapley understood Bradley's creative side and admired his talents. The two became lifelong friends.

After graduating from high school in 1854, Bradley planned to study **drafting**. He wanted to attend the Lawrence Scientific School at Harvard University. But first, he had to earn some money.

At the time, many young women were moving to the city to take factory jobs. They lived in **rooming houses**. But many of these women were lonesome for home.

Bradley noticed that they often wrote letters to their friends and family members. So he began to sell **stationery**. He sold it door-to-door at the rooming houses. This was Bradley's first experience as an **entrepreneur**. He was good at it, and he loved being his own boss. By the fall of 1854, Bradley had earned enough money to start college.

In the mid-1800s, only about 1 percent of US males had a college degree. But Bradley was eager to learn **drafting** skills and earn a degree of his own. However, before he could finish, his parents moved again. Bradley went with them to Hartford, Connecticut. He never earned a degree.

Bradley's former university is now called the Harvard School of Engineering and Applied Sciences.

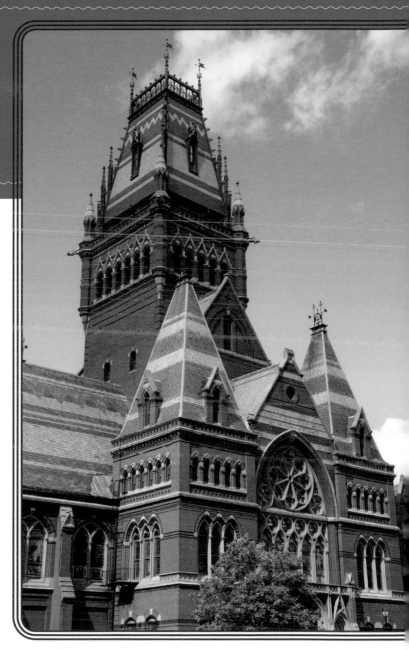

Chapter 3

EARLY CAREER

After moving to Hartford, Bradley looked for a job. But he couldn't find one that interested him. So in 1856, he took a train to Springfield, Massachusetts, to look for work. There, the Wason Manufacturing Company manufactured train cars and **streetcars**. The company hired Bradley as a **draftsman**.

At his new job, Bradley was responsible for designing a luxury train car for the **viceroy** of Egypt. It turned out beautifully, and Bradley was given a **lithograph** of the finished car. He was so excited by the gift that he decided to learn lithography.

Shortly after, Bradley went to

The Wason Manufacturing Company created passenger coaches to travel the First Transcontinental Railroad.

FUN FACT

Trains were a common form of transportation during Bradley's youth. The first gasoline-powered automobile was not invented until he was about 50 years old.

Rhode Island to visit his friend Tapley. While there, Bradley completed a **lithography apprenticeship**. In 1860, he started the Milton Bradley Company.

Bradley's new company printed items for Springfield businesses. One day, he was asked to create a lithograph of a presidential candidate. That candidate was Abraham Lincoln. The lithograph sold well at first. But when Lincoln grew a beard, the prints were worthless. The loss nearly forced Bradley to close his business. But he was **undaunted**. He would soon come up with an exciting new idea!

Bradley's lithograph of Abraham Lincoln. People had trouble recognizing Lincoln without his distinctive beard and hat.

Chapter 4
The Checkered
GAME OF LIFE

Bradley was always thinking of new uses for his **lithograph** machine. In the summer of 1860, he visited Tapley again. One night, they played a board game that had been imported from England. Suddenly, the idea that started the Milton Bradley empire struck! Bradley realized he had the supplies to manufacture his own board game. His lithograph machine could print the game, cards, instructions, and packaging. All he needed now was an original game idea.

Bradley thought of a game that he would name The Checkered Game of Life. The word *checkered* can describe a checkerboard pattern. But it can also mean having ups and downs, good and bad.

The game board Bradley created looked like a typical red and black checkerboard. And the game's theme was the ups and downs of life. The object

FUN FACT

Milton Bradley also wrote and **patented** the rules for the game of croquet.

Bradley's
original
game board

THE CHECKERED GAME OF LIFE.

of the game
was to get to
"Happy Old
Age" and not
"Ruin."

In late 1860, Bradley's
company began creating copies of The Checkered
Game of Life. He showed the game to distributors in New York
City. They loved it, and Bradley's finances were saved from ruin. This
financial security enabled Bradley to marry his sweetheart Vilona Larue
Eaton later that year.

Chapter 5

The Making of a BOARD GAME

3 The model game is tested and **revised** based on advice from players.

2 The game creator sketches the game on paper and makes a working model.

4 A designer creates a look for the game board. Once the game creator approves the look, the designer prepares final artwork for the print shop.

1 Every board game starts as an idea. The game needs a theme, an object, and mechanics. The theme is what the game is about. The object is what determines the winner. And the mechanics are how the game is played.

START

FUN FACT

The early Milton Bradley board games used an eight-sided wooden top instead of dice. Dice were associated with gambling and bad moral character.

7

Packaging is created for the game. Usually the package is a box. The cardboard used is sturdy but not as thick as the game board itself.

6

Additional game pieces are produced. These can include money, cards, instructions, and other items. Some are printed. Others, such as dice or small objects, are purchased from a supplier.

8

An **assembly line** packages the game pieces and then puts the game board, instructions, and pieces into the box. The assembly line workers can be humans or robots.

5

Thick cardboard is prepared to become a game board. It has creases or shallow cuts so the board can fold. The printed game board is mounted on this cardboard.

9

The completed games are boxed in larger containers and shipped to stores, where people buy them. At home, the new game is opened and the fun begins!

END

Chapter 6
Ups and Downs
OF REAL LIFE

The Checkered Game of Life became popular very quickly. Bradley received orders from all over the country. During the winter of 1860, he sold more than 45,000 copies! But Bradley's focus changed when the **Civil War** began in April 1861.

After the war began, many young men were being killed daily in battle. People were not thinking much about games. But they were thinking about ways to support the soldiers. Citizens and businesses became focused on the war effort.

Bradley took a break from producing games and used his **drafting** skills to design weapons. However, this work soon brought Bradley back to making games. He met some soldiers stationed in Springfield. When they weren't on active duty, the

FUN FACT

During World War II, Milton Bradley Company reproduced a version of the Civil War game kit. It was very successful.

Soldiers from the 12th Regiment relax in their barracks. Bradley's game kit was a much-needed distraction in difficult times.

men were lonesome and bored. Bradley thought playing games would fill the long hours and cheer them up. He decided to produce a kit of games for the soldiers. Among the games were chess, checkers, and The Checkered Game of Life. Charities bought thousands of kits to distribute to the soldiers.

While successful in business, Bradley suffered a personal loss during this time. His wife Vilona died. The two did not have any children.

More change came for Bradley in 1864, when J. F. Tapley and Clark W. Bryan became his business partners. After the war ended in 1865, Bradley turned back to board games. It was time to have some fun again.

Chapter 7

Beyond the BOARD GAME

Once he returned to creating games, Bradley happily spent hours making sketches. He liked using his imagination. After sketching, Bradley built models to test his ideas. His training in **drafting** helped him understand how things worked. Better yet, he could build things from his own imagination.

In 1865, Bradley invented The Myriopticon. It was a box with a crank that

Friedrich Froebel inspired Bradley to improve the United States' education system.

displayed printed illustrations on a screen. It even came with a script. The kit was a popular Christmas gift that year.

Four years later, in 1869, Bradley married schoolteacher Ellen "Nellie" Thayer. That same year, he attended a lecture about a new idea in education. The kindergarten movement started in Germany and was guided by Friedrich Froebel. Froebel believed that young children could learn by doing creative activities. Bradley remembered how his own father had made learning fun. He loved Froebel's idea and became **passionate** about bringing kindergarten to the United States.

Chapter 8
Bradley Goes to KINDERGARTEN

Milton Bradley Company continued to make popular board games. But with Bradley's new **passion**, the company had a new **market** to develop. His enthusiasm about kindergarten led the company to begin producing educational supplies.

One such product was inspired by a set of kindergarten learning tools called gifts. These were wooden blocks and shapes developed by Froebel and used for creative play. Art supplies were also important to the kindergarten idea. Milton Bradley Company started producing gifts and colored paper. Bradley spent months developing the exact colors to use in his products.

At first, kindergartens were only in large cities. But Bradley wanted every child to have a fun introduction to learning. He traveled the

FUN FACT

Bradley enjoyed painting with watercolors.

Modern toy blocks are very similar to Bradley's gifts.

country demonstrating his educational supplies. He often gave supplies away for free to encourage opening kindergartens. He didn't want children to miss out just because schools couldn't afford new supplies.

Bradley and Nellie started the first kindergarten in Springfield. They were both teachers there. This allowed Bradley to test new learning products with the children.

Chapter 9

The Changing GAME OF LIFE

As Bradley worked to fulfill his **passion** for toys and education in the 1870s, a **recession** hit the United States. Most people did not have much money. They tried to buy only what they needed.

During this time, sales of games and educational supplies dropped. Bradley's company struggled to stay profitable. But Bradley continued giving away supplies. He was so passionate about helping schools that he wasn't thinking about making money.

Bradley's investors were worried, however. They gave Bradley an **ultimatum**. The company had to stop producing kindergarten supplies or they would quit. But Bradley wouldn't budge. So Bradley's longtime friend Tapley bought the investors' shares. Tapley also took over

FUN FACT

In 1880, Milton Bradley Company began producing jigsaw puzzles. One successful line of puzzles featured wrecked vehicles.

Because of the recession, the US stock market closed in 1873. Many people lost money and panicked.

as company president. He encouraged Bradley to continue working on school supplies and game design.

Around this time, Bradley and Nellie had two children. Florence was born in 1876. Lillian Alice was born in 1881.

Chapter 10

SUCCESS
and Satisfaction

By 1900, the **recession** was over and Bradley's board games were selling well. These sales kept Bradley's business going, as sales of school supplies were not going as well.

Kindergartens had become popular in the United States. And Bradley had been **instrumental** in making this happen. Many classrooms used his company's supplies. Despite this, the school supply line was not profitable. But Bradley continued to make supplies and promote color in the classroom.

Bradley published teacher magazines containing stories, news, and advertisements.

FUN FACT

Bradley designed a
color wheel to help
teach art in classrooms.

Art supplies available at the time were expensive. They were meant for professional artists. Schools could not afford to buy such high-priced items.

Bradley saw this as an exciting opportunity. He developed inexpensive watercolor paints and wax crayons for schools. He also wrote helpful books about using art and color in education. Teachers could read these books and discover ways to use Bradley's art supplies.

Bradley also wanted his educational supplies to be easily available. The US Post Office was now delivering mail even to rural communities. Milton Bradley Company made good use of this service. It was one of the first companies to **market** products in a **mail-order** catalog. Bradley's supplies were no longer just affordable. They were convenient to purchase!

Chapter 11

THE END GAME

Bradley retired from the everyday business of Milton Bradley Company at 70 years of age. But the company was in good hands. Tapley was still its president. His son, William Tapley, took Bradley's place on the board of directors. And Bradley continued to contribute new ideas to the company.

Meanwhile, Milton Bradley Company kept growing. The headquarters in Springfield expanded to nine buildings that filled an entire city block.

Bradley died on May 11, 1911. His life's work was done, but he would never be forgotten. His name has become **synonymous** with great board games.

Bradley had never really cared about fame or fortune. He just wanted to make learning fun for young children. He also wanted to bring people together over amusing games. Like the winning phrase in his original creation, Bradley lived to "Happy Old Age" in his own game of life.

FUN FACT

Bradley was inducted into the National Toy Hall of Fame almost 100 years after his death.

Milton Bradley Company will always have a place in Springfield's history.

Chapter 12

Milton Bradley's
WORK LIVES ON

Bradley didn't live long enough to see all his dreams realized. By the 1920s, kindergartens were included in almost all US elementary schools. Milton Bradley Company had become the leading manufacturer and seller of educational materials. And thanks to Bradley, kindergarten classrooms displayed colorful artwork.

Candy Land is just one of Milton Bradley Company's classic games.

In 1960, Bradley's original game was rereleased to celebrate its one-hundredth birthday. The game

FUN FACT

Milton Bradley's Battleship was adapted from a pencil-and-paper game created around the time of World War I.

was redesigned and renamed The Game of Life. Much later, in 1984, the Hasbro Company bought Milton Bradley Company. It kept the Milton Bradley **brand** and continued to create new games.

Today, the Milton Bradley brand is still going strong. Its games continue to delight children and adults. And they all follow Bradley's vision for people to have fun together.   Milton Bradley's imagination, **passion**, and skills have made a lasting contribution. Today, people around the world can enjoy the rewards of his inventions and accomplishments.

HOW MANY OF THESE MILTON BRADLEY GAMES DO YOU RECOGNIZE?

- Ants in the Pants
- Battleship
- Candy Land
- Don't Break the Ice
- Hungry Hungry Hippos
- Jenga
- Operation
- Scattergories
- Trouble
- Twister
- Yahtzee

TIMELINE

1836

Milton Bradley is born in Vienna, Maine, on November 8.

1860

Milton Bradley Company is founded as a lithography business. Bradley creates The Checkered Game of Life.

1854

Bradley studies drafting at Harvard.

1861

The Civil War begins. Milton Bradley Company produces a game kit for soldiers.

1869

Bradley becomes interested in the kindergarten movement. Milton Bradley Company begins producing educational materials.

1960

The Checkered Game of Life board game is rereleased as The Game of Life.

1911

Milton Bradley dies on May 11.

1984

Hasbro, Inc. acquires Milton Bradley Company.

Glossary

apprenticeship – an arrangement where a person learns a trade or a craft from a skilled worker.

assembly line – a way of making something in which the item moves from worker to worker until it is finished.

brand – a category of products made by a particular company and all having the same company name.

Civil War – the war between the United States of America and the Confederate States of America from 1861 to 1865.

drafting – a profession that involves making detailed drawings and plans for things such as machines and structures. A person who does this is called a draftsman.

entrepreneur – one who organizes, manages, and accepts the risks of a business or an enterprise.

Industrial Revolution – a period starting in England in the mid-1700s, later spreading to America. It marked the change from agricultural to industrial societies.

instrumental – important in helping or causing something to occur.

lithograph – a picture created through the process of printing from a smooth, flat stone or a metal plate. On this surface, the picture or the design holds printing ink. The rest of the surface does not.

mail order – a method of buying goods that are sent to the buyer through the mail.

market – a particular type of people who might buy something. To market a product is to advertise or promote it so people will want to buy it.

WEBSITES

To learn more about Toy Trailblazers, visit **booklinks.abdopublishing.com**. These links are routinely monitored and updated to provide the most current information available.

passion – something one feels very strongly about. Someone who expresses strong feelings about something is passionate.

patent – to apply for and receive the exclusive right to make or sell an invention. This right lasts for a certain period of time.

recession – a period of time when business activity slows.

revise – to change something in order to correct or improve it.

revolutionary – causing or relating to a great or complete change.

rooming house – a private house in which rooms are rented either temporarily or permanently.

stationery – writing materials such as paper, pens, and ink.

streetcar – a vehicle that travels on tracks on city streets.

synonymous – strongly suggesting a particular idea, person, or quality is closely associated with something.

textile mill – a building where woven fabric is created.

ultimatum – a promise or threat that something will be done if someone else does not do what is wanted.

undaunted – not afraid to continue doing something even when problems or difficulties arise.

viceroy – a person who rules as the representative of a king or a queen.

Index